T0050999

If you were a PLUS SIGN

by Trisha Speed Shaskan
illustrated by Francesca Carabelli

PICTURE WINDOW BOOKS
Minneapolis, Minnesota

plus sign (+) a symbol used to show addition

Editor: Christianne Jones
Designers: Nathan Gassman and Hilary Wacholz
Page Production: Melissa Kes
The illustrations in this book were created with acrylics.

Picture Window Books
1710 Roe Crest Drive
North Mankato, MN 56003
www.capstonepub.com

Copyright © 2009 by Picture Window Books, a Capstone imprint. All rights reserved. No part of this book may be reproduced without written permission from the publisher. The publisher takes no responsibility for the use of any of the materials or methods described in this book, nor for the products thereof.

Library of Congress Cataloging-in-Publication Data
Shaskan, Trisha Speed, 1973-
If you were a plus sign / by Trisha Speed Shaskan ; illustrated by Francesca Carabelli.
p. cm. — (Math fun)
Includes index.
ISBN 978-1-4048-4784-2 (library binding)
ISBN 978-1-4048- 4785-9 (paperback)
1. Mathematical notation—Juvenile literature.
2. Addition—Juvenile literature. I. Carabelli, Francesca, ill. II. Title.
QA41.S482 2009
513.2'11—dc22 *2008006458*

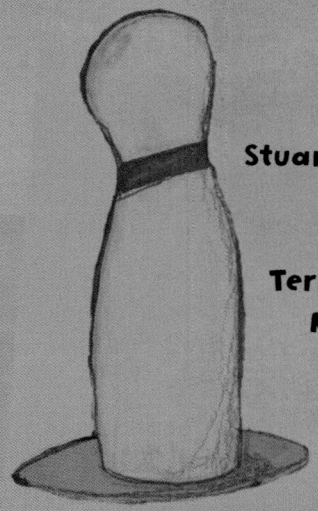

Special thanks to our advisers for their expertise:

Stuart Farm, M.Ed., Mathematics Lecturer
University of North Dakota

Terry Flaherty, Ph.D., Professor of English
Minnesota State University, Mankato

Printed in the United States 6012

If you were a plus sign . . .

... you would help add things together.

Ida plus Ike equals true love.
They make a family of two.

Ida and Ike have a cub called Ina.
They make a family of three.
2+1=3
Ida, Ike, and Ina love pets. They have two seals.
They make a family of five.
3
+2
5

If you were a plus sign, you would be a symbol used to show addition. You would be part of an addition problem.

Selma juggles five red balls plus two green balls. That's a total of seven balls.

$$\begin{array}{r} 5 \\ +\,2 \\ \hline 7 \end{array}$$

Trigg jumps through four blue hoops plus four purple hoops. That's a total of eight hoops.
4 + 4 = 8

If you were a plus sign, you would be used like the word "and."

Pluck gives Doodle one
valentine and eight chocolates.
One and eight equals nine.
1+8=9

Five bulldogs met five tigers to play basketball at the park. They made a sum of ten players.

Six bulldogs plus six tigers showed up to cheer them on. They made a sum of twelve cheerleaders.

$$\begin{array}{r} 6 \\ +\,6 \\ \hline 12 \end{array}$$

If you were a plus sign, you could work left to right or top to bottom.

Spotty cooks four blueberry pancakes for herself and three plain pancakes for Dotty.

Spotty stacks the three plain pancakes and the four blueberry pancakes on a plate.

If you were a plus sign, you could add in any order and still get the same sum.

A frightened frog leaps across four lily pads and then bounces onto two more lily pads. He jumps on six lily pads altogether.

4+2=6

A frightened frog leaps across two lily pads
and then bounces onto four more lily pads.
He jumps on six lily pads altogether.
2
+ 4
6

If you were a plus sign, you could add any amount of numbers. You could add two, three, four, or more. You would get the same sum no matter how the numbers were arranged.

Five elephants plus four hippos plus three rhinos equals twelve show animals.

$$5+4+3=12$$

Five elephants plus three rhinos plus four hippos equals twelve show animals.

If you were a plus sign, you could add small numbers or big numbers.

Gert wears eight red bracelets on her right arm and eight pink bracelets on her left arm. Gert is wearing sixteen bracelets.

8+8=16

Gert has thirteen bows on her tail and fourteen bows in her mane. She's wearing twenty-seven bows.

13+14=27

Gert has 100 polka dots on her skirt, and Stretch has 100 triangles on his vest and tie. Together, they have two hundred shapes on their clothes.

100+100=200

If you were a plus sign, you could help solve story problems.

Cherry juggles five red balls. She adds three green balls and two orange balls. How many balls does Cherry juggle in all?

$$5+3+2=10$$

Cherry juggles ten balls in all.

You would always help add things together ...

... if you were a *plus* sign.

Addition Review

It's time to use that plus sign and review! Throughout the book you have added a lot of different items. Now grab a piece of paper and a pencil. Solve the addition problems below.

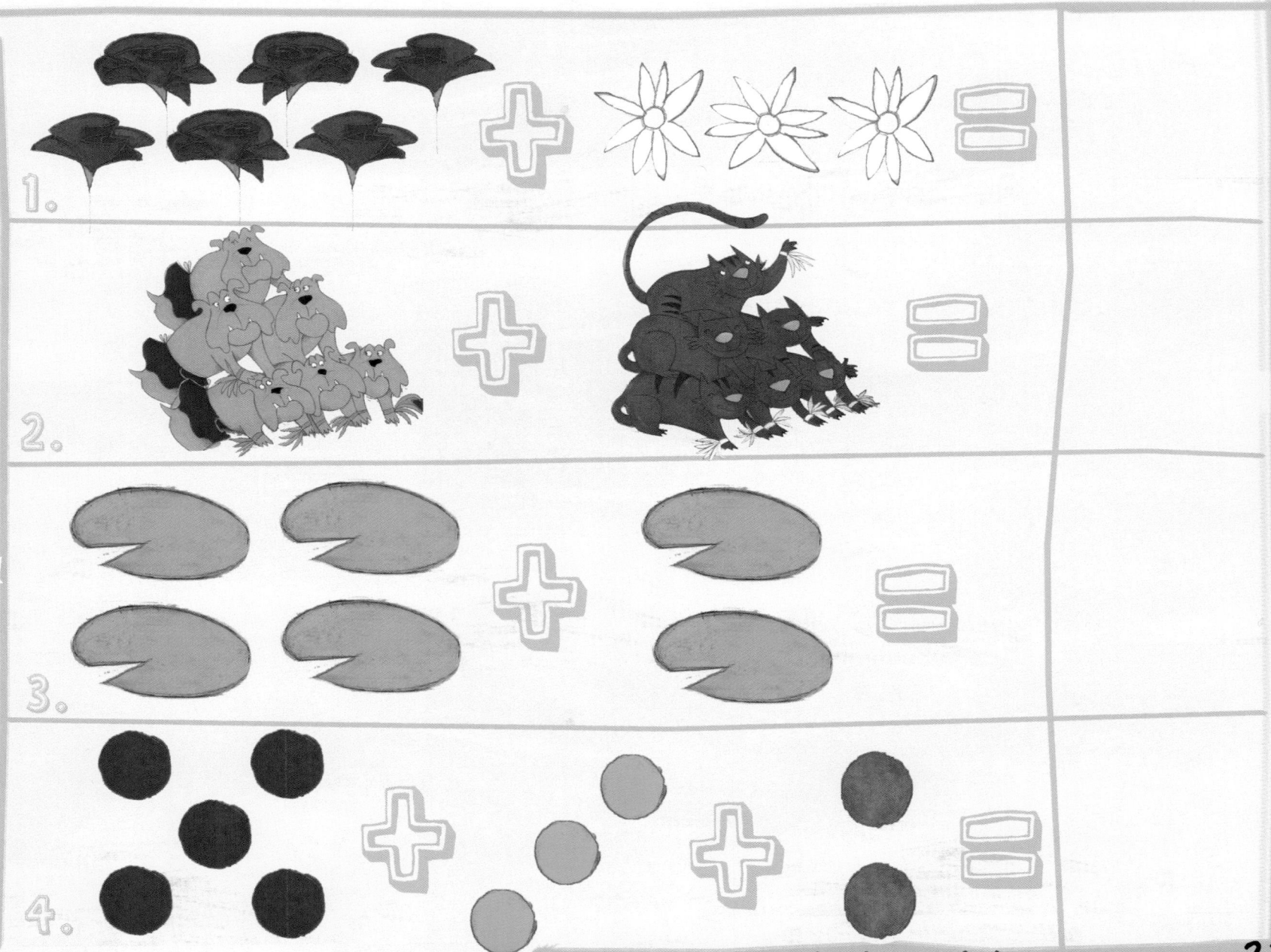

Answers: 1. (9) 2. (12) 3. (6) 4. (10)

Glossary

add—to find the sum of two or more numbers
addition—the act of adding numbers together
plus sign—a symbol used to show addition
sum—the number you get when you add two or more numbers together
symbol—a sign that stands for something else

To Learn More

More Books to Read

Bauer, David. *Adding Arctic Animals.* Bloomington, Minn.: Yellow Umbrella Books, 2004.

Cleary, Brian P. *The Mission of Addition.* Minneapolis: Millbrook Press, 2005.

Gisler, David. *Addition Annie.* New York: Children's Press, 2002.

On the Web

FactHound offers a safe, fun way to find Web sites related to topics in this book. All of the sites on FactHound have been researched by our staff.

1. Visit *www.facthound.com*
2. Type in this special code: 1404847847
3. Click on the FETCH IT button.

Your trusty FactHound will fetch the best sites for you!

Index

adding
- big numbers, 18
- different number amounts, 16
- in order, 14
- left to right, 12
- small numbers, 18
- top to bottom, 12

plus sign
- definition, 6
- used as "and," 8

story problems, 20
sum, 10

Look for all of the books in the Math Fun series:

If You Were a Fraction
If You Were a Minus Sign
If You Were a Plus Sign
If You Were a Set
If You Were an Even Number
If You Were an Odd Number